SOUND THEATRE

David Pownall

Sound Theatre

Thoughts on the radio play

OBERON BOOKS
LONDON

First published in 2011 by Oberon Books Ltd
521 Caledonian Road, London N7 9RH
Tel: 020 7607 3637 / Fax: 020 7607 3629
e-mail: info@oberonbooks.com
www.oberonbooks.com

A catalogue record for this book is available from the British Library.

ISBN: 978-1-84943-102-6

Printed in Great Britain by CPI Antony Rowe, Chippenham

Contents

Chapter I

IT'S THE FIRST reading of the radio play – generally agreed by everyone concerned, except the author, to be a matter of limited importance. But for the maker of the piece it is a big moment – the first time he's heard the play run together outside his own head. The studio-wise actors will be holding back, not commiting themselves to a full performance before they've heard what their colleagues are going to come up with. If there's a starry name in the cast there may be some suggestive incoherence while the ego gets into the shadow of the part. The director is concentrating on whether he has cast the voices accurately. Is there enough differentiation? Do any of them sound like each other? At the back of his mind is an anonymous pair of ears prone to confusion.

The director has read the play many times, probably more than the author. He knows that the model of interpretation in his mind will only work if the mix of voices is right. No one picks up on the author's anxiety. This can be so acute that some playwrights don't attend recordings, preferring to trust to luck. This is not a good idea. Always, always be there, even if you sit in the control room for three days without saying anything. I only ever missed one recording of a play of mine, and that was because I was on the other side of the world. Upon my return I rang the director and asked how everything had gone. What I was told sent a chill down my spine. The actors had had a wonderful time with the play. And how.

In terms of tension, at the recording of a radio play the author starts in at the level of a stage dress rehearsal. Immediately after the first reading what was whole is broken up into scenes and sections and probably not recorded in order. You know that after this run-through there will be no strung-together homogeneity in the experience until the play is broadcast. The interpretation in studio can tilt and slide to one side – maybe not the side you favour. If it does, what are you going to do about it? Never let a critical thought go unsaid, but be sure you can back it up. So, put up or shut up.

* * *

Radio theatre depends on getting inside the head and staying there. But the body and its personal atmospheres are not forgotten. The sound of breathing, the colours of accents, vocal delivery, the quirks of emphasis, these run parallel in importance to words themselves. To a skilled radio actor, the microphone is a transplant bolted into the bones of his head.

Some of the best directors of radio theatre were stage actors. They tend to focus on performance more than soundscape.

Whatever will be achieved in realising a play will come from the state of the actor in studio during the very brief time available to realise the play – two days for an hour-long recording. This isn't much time for an actor to get his teeth into a part, so technique is important. It is possible that the actor will have only read the play properly on the way to the studio. At the first reading – which is the supreme moment for the playwright – any superficiality of approach will show and the pressure will be on.

An actor with a voice that is recognised as a beautiful *instrument*, may surf through the reading, riding on reputation. The director and the playwright will clock the fact. How, in the time available, can this be remedied? In the evening an actor may be working at a theatre, doing a big part. He's saving himself, eking out his energy. That's easier to deal with. The microphone picks up energy levels. The right kind of pressure has to be put on the actor without him knowing it.

* * *

The studio manager on the control panel is very experienced. Everything she hears affects her, which means she has ideas and opinions that cross into the territory of the director. What the actors say and how they say it is as much sound to the studio manager as the effects. She considers her job to be recording the very best sound available. She cannot divide her world into proper spheres of responsibility and leave the director to his. When an actor is getting it wrong it is as painful to her as a fault on the equipment. She also has a technician's ulterior disrespect for the whole idea of directing. During the last few hours of the day's work resentment surfaces and erupts. She has to be slapped down. Her sensitivity in keeping control of what is being recorded suffers. The director criticises her, refusing to avoid the confrontation. Eventually, after error upon error, he asks her to go out into the corridor and they have a row that makes a nonsense of the studio soundproofing. They return to the control room and resume recording. Within a quarter of an hour the whole episode is history.

* * *

The third scene is not going well. We're down to the inflexion of one line. The actor can't get it right. The director has explained what he wants several times but hasn't got through. The line has already been recorded several times and scrapped. When played back to him, the actor can hear what's wrong – but the way to do it properly escapes him. Somehow he can't get his mind round the intonation that's needed. To hit that right note with perfect judgement can be difficult, causing embarrassment to the most experienced.

We're well behind on the recording schedule. That will have to be made up somehow. Because of the severity of the budget, overtime is out of the question.

Now the actor is getting tired of being put on the spot. Everyone is aware of a crisis looming – the control room, the green room and the studio itself. There is an *atmosphere.*

Atmospheres are of critical importance to a radio play. The playwright specifies what is needed – sitting-room atmos, pub atmos, underwater atmos, country lane atmos, pigsty, pillar-box, perambulator, palace atmos, but never a tension atmos outside what the work requires. It will always be picked up. Both the human and technical equipment is hyper-sensitive.

As a problem the one line seems diminutive, a few words. Why not move on, gloss over it? But Martin, the director is a terrier. He never gives up because he knows it will flaw the piece. What he won't do is speak the line himself as he wants it done – even though he was once an actor and has a wealth of experience. If a performance is tilted by heavy advice on interpretation, the emphasis of the part will shift and the whole sound impression of a human character will become uneasy and ill-defined.

Essential directorial design comes at the time of casting – putting the right voice in the part, backed by the right acting skill. That's when the director hears the play in his head. This is the conception that looms over every sound recorded.

Over twenty years of making plays with Martin, watching him rock backwards and forwards as the sound is recorded, eyes shut, head in hands, you know that he's listening to two versions of the scene simultaneously, one in his mind, the other in his ear. The first is assessing the second, comparing.

The actor in trouble is getting resentful. He's getting too much attention. To give everyone time to ease up, a tea break is called. The actor knows this is for his benefit. He's being given time to think the whole thing through. He goes into the corridor with his script and stares at the line, concentrating. He understands it. He knows the character. Why can't he say it as it needs to be said? If he was saying it badly on stage it could be disguised with business, the fault made not so obvious. But here, because the word is all we have, and every word matters, there's no prop to be toyed with as cover, no mask to wear, no hiding place.

The actor is alone with his voice. Today might be the time when extraneous problems are pressing down, allowing the voice below the voice to emerge, the voice of the youth, the boy, the voice before the theatre made its claim. The best radio actors are exceptionally clever with impersonation – give them a short while and they'll come up with anything you want. The speed and skill displayed can be astonishing. But under stress the original voice sometimes emerges – perhaps in a dialect that was the raw material preceeding the elocution lessons and voice classes at drama school.

CHAPTER I

When received pronunciation slips away and the western side of Peterborough or dockside Newcastle emerges, it is a choice moment of language, a complex inner music that a playwright enjoys. After all, it is a story with potential – the comedy of pretension or the tragedy of loss of identity. When I worked in newly-independent Zambia during the Sixties I watched a tragic version unfold. As the country became free, a young African newsreader with a superb cut-glass English accent began his career on television. His beautiful voice and poise – and Savile Row suit – became wildly popular, even amongst the tough party organisers and strong-arm men. He somehow carved a special place for himself in the national consciousness. Here, look at this, he was saying to the ex-colonial masters, we can do anything you can do, we can even *be* you.

Out of the blue, he committed suicide.

* * *

The old actor is telling one of his stories, dropping the names of luminaries from the great days of twentieth-century theatre. It's the end of the tea break. The director – who knew them all as well – looks at his watch. He needs to get on. The recording schedule has been knocked about by delays – particularly the one line that must be got right. He gently interrupts the old actor's story. Time to get back to work. As the director goes in search of the man with the problem, he knows in his heart that the line will never be exactly as he wants it. He's a perfectionist, and that's a hard thing to be when the form punishes imperfection so harshly.

* * *

Two lead actors in something of mine were extraordinarly good as husband and wife tearing each other apart in a tortuous marriage. When the recording was over the man gave me a lift to a party we had both been invited to. I complimented him on his performance and how well he had worked with the actress, finding the emotional depths of the troubled relationship. "Thank you, David" he said. "We were greatly helped by having lived together for five years."

* * *

The integrity of the text is still an item in radio drama. People worry about it, employ their powers to defend it. The special pleasure playwrights derive from working in the medium – an experience brief, intense and relatively trouble-free compared to the other technical forms derived from theatre – is based on this respect. No one mentions sanctity, but there is a feeling that should the text be mangled no good will come of it.

When ten minutes needs to be cut from a play because scenes have stretched while being recorded and it's going to overrun the slot, the director turns to the playwright. The text has been timed – first by the one who wrote it, reading it through on his own against the clock, secondly on the computer word- and line-count, using the running-time of previous completed plays as a database, thirdly by the director in preparation for the recording, fourthly by the director's PA at the first read-through with the cast.

As scene follows scene during the recording, organic shifts and changes occur. In spite of all the checks and estimates, the relationships between the voices pull the timing. The interaction between each actor's personal pattern of expression, the shadowy pauses and rhythms, all add or subtract seconds that build into an amount confounding the estimates.

Out of experience, the playwright bears this inevitable need for alterations in mind. There are no laws governing the time a script takes to play. An eye is kept on certain scenes from the first read-through onwards. What the director sees as a good cut can be butchery to the playwright, who is on a different level, still bound by the structure originally put in place.

Cutting requires flair and fortitude at this stage. At the time of the edit, when the playwright is usually not present, the director needs to be able to make contact on the phone to discuss final tweaks and adjustments.

Also there is the opposite of cutting. The dead-room, where there is no atmosphere at all and the silence is profound, is a good place to send a playwright when another ten minutes of script is needed before the recording can finish. When first written, the play appeared to be in perfect balance. But the transmission time allocated to the play dictates. Padding and panic stand naked on radio. Any play can be stopped in its tracks if the listener detects a nervy, slackening hold on what's happening.

With the action of the piece running clearly in the mind, and a greater knowledge of the characters being played, cutting, adding and adjustment not only feel natural but exhilarating. To this must be added the odd chess-game of recording scenes out of sequence, which means that the playwright must have a strong mental hold over the play. Recording out of sequence is done to save money and time if different scenes take place in the same atmosphere, or all the scenes in which an expensive actor is needed are recorded one after the other to reduce the number of days he's needed for.

No one ever mocks the playwright's readiness to change the text. No producer is standing on the sidelines asking for a bit more of this and a bit more of that. Writing on the spot within the process of recording the play is an inherent part of working with sound only, which is an intimate part of the dimension of time. A new scene written under pressure can shift the heart of the play and teach the playwright the truth of what he was trying to say.

CHAPTER I

Sound theatre is a performance art of special purity, cousin to music. It happens in the receptive mind with no help from flashier aids to entertainment. No sequins get down the microphone. No make-up. No stunning frocks. No gurning. No knowing winks. No nudity. No cavorting eye-candy. If the voice is right, on radio the ugliest woman in the world can play Helen of Troy.

Words, noise, silence, followable thought – that's all there is to work with. Artists of sound theatre can make it mean anything and everything.

* * *

Chapter II

If you're averse to audience participation, don't turn on the radio if a play is being broadcast. For you, as listener, there's plenty of work to be done.

Turning on the radio is something we do when we go into a room or get into the car and feel inclined to listen, often speculatively. The programme we first hit can be anything. If you hear canned laughter you'll know it can't be a play, even a play designed to make you laugh. That's the dividing line between a show and a play. A show cannot survive without a response from an audience, canned or live. On radio, a play has to do without any assistance of this kind. It is suspended in a universe of its own, a cloud of starry verbal vapour.

There are a few recordings of *The Goon Show* that were made without canned laughter or studio audience. The difference it makes to the surreal humour is remarkable. Cast into the silent air the text has a strange, floating pureness. When you laugh you are alone.

We always hear radio plays alone, even if we're sitting in the same room with other people. Unlike theatre, a social art, there is no togetherness to be had.

The idea of a large audience in one place listening to a radio play is alien. The audience for sound theatre has no collective entity, being made up of millions of minds using independent imaginations guided by the play. Clearly, these minds are all open at the time of broadcast, but they are not in contact with each other. Wherever you travel in the action you are making the journey in the human mind and its knowledge of the real world. That is how this form of drama works, how the story has to be told – created for the mind only, the part of us that responds to language, and inner powers.

A reader with a book can be said to be in a similar position, lifting the story off the page by personal effort, making it live by use of one imagination – the author's – working within the other – the reader's. But anyone who has adapted a novel for radio, or has had one adapted, knows there is a major difference. Essentially, a radio play is dialogue. Every aspect of the novel has to be conveyed through speech. If monologue is employed it is because the first choice, dialogue, is too slow if psychological ground has to be covered quickly. But the challenge in writing radio plays is to achieve everything possible by dialogue. A way must be found for all the descriptive passages to be rendered through verbal interaction between characters. A book of a hundred thousand words will be distilled down to ten thousand.

* * *

Radio plays usually last from three-quarters of an hour, to one hour, even to two hours, in some rare cases. There was a time when there was some accordance between the length of stage plays and radio plays, but that was during an era when the theatre and the BBC kept much closer together.

Even a play of forty-five minutes assumes considerable concentration spans on the part of the listener. At the beginning there must be a real hope that it will be worthwhile. People don't embark on listening to radio drama because they're fatigued and fancy a mindless hour or so on the sofa. I've never heard anyone say they'll sit down and listen to bad radio the same way they'll sit down to watch bad television.

To get up and leave the room during a radio play means losing track of a work being created by the listener as well as the artists who made it. There's a fallacy that one can always slot back into a plot after leaving it for a while, as people of fashion did in the theatre during previous centuries. What you end up with is incomplete, but completeness may not matter to you. If a revelation occurred while you were absent, what you will go away with may be the opposite of what was intended, which does matter to the playwright.

* * *

Audience has become a big business word for dedicated consumers who know what they want. In politics it is used as a synonym for the electorate. We apply it to every form of creative expression, every artistic endeavour, even though hearing, what it refers to (Latin – *audio*, to hear), has no part in the appreciation of some art. My 1849 Latin dictionary adds *perceive* to the meaning of *audio*, e.g. *I see what you're saying.* Isn't this, in essence, archaic? Would we, overlaid by images, use sight as a synonym for understanding?

Sculpture and painting can do without our ears, but they need an audience. Even accountancy harks back to hearing – *auditor*, one who hears monastic accounts being read out. So, at the back of our atavistic mind, hearing has always had eyes. The skald, the storyteller and the chief's praise-singer depended on the magic of the spoken word and its power to open up all the senses within the mind.

The radio playwright is the descendant of these bards.

* * *

The theatre of sound relies as much on the creative receptiveness of the listener as the playwright's words. No other form of artistic expression has such a close bond. When a radio play succeeds, the connection between playwright and listener has been charged with the energy of two imaginations sharing the same scenes, action and characters. When it fails, one imagination has taken leave of the other.

The makers of the piece do not have all the power. The listener in the armchair, the motorway driver stuck in a traffic-jam at Newport Pagnell, may appear inert and passive, but they are both generators.

Nothing can be achieved without the second imagination supplementing the first. The room made in the listener's mind for the play is uniquely valuable – more so than in other artistic experiences. That room in the listener's mind is by no means empty. When it comes to subjectivity, radio theatre practitioners know that what they're up against is people hearing what they want to hear, never mind the script, never mind the experience the playwright thought was being passed on. That deep involvement of self is the maze the play must be threaded through, and remaining in touch with the tradition of speech and exchange within that self.

Over the last ninety years a mechanism has developed inside the very nature of radio listening that is locked in the pleasures of stability and unchangeableness. The reasons will be gone into later, but for present purposes it is worth noting that it is only a mechanism, and mechanisms can be dismantled.

The standing of the radio play has been stuck in this conservatism, and while languishing there has been battered by the storms a great broadcasting empire has to weather. Radio theatre lies as much in the shadow of soap opera today as film and television, and has done right from the beginning, shepherded towards domestic melodrama rather than an evolving serious theatre. What has been achieved in the latter often came from playwrights, novelists and poets not brought up in radio writing but recognised and transferred from the other disciplines.

Nothing in film and television has achieved the intense linguistic perfection of the best radio theatre. Neither have they the potential that could yet bring radio drama, if liberated, to its fulfilment. Half of its natural environment in the mind remains unexplored.

* * *

Chapter III

WRITING THEATRE THAT is only to be heard encourages a certain canniness of mind. The very fact of vision being absent adds a dimension rather than takes one away.

The light that shines out of words travelling through the mind has no name in aesthetics. When a play is born in the head and will be performed only in the head it has a unique character, stripped down to the music of syllables and the business of understanding.

Because the great weight and complexity of the world is lifted off the shoulders of language when it is freed from the physical, words walk more freely, trip over less often, and mean more.

Writing for the ear means moving at pace through whatever country the story opens up. It is the best mode of authorship for close, intimate investigation, good for showing people making too much use of each other; the outer regions of ambition, emotional servitude, absurd despair, personality-wrestling, interviewing gods, excitement acting as an intoxicant, quiet kinds of madness that take time to reveal themselves, detailed anatomies of greed, *hauteur* and vanity, thought processes that come out of nowhere and take over nations, moral abasement, believing your own lies, incomprehensible love, intricate revenge, and once-thought impossible forms of political shame.

The list is almost as long as the language.

* * *

This book is a personal response to a form of theatre that, in spite of the sophistication and rate of advance of its technology, never gets too distant from storytelling. It is no attempt to write a history of the radio play. The need for a scholar to provide an up-to-date, in-depth survey remains. Some history fragments are here because history is so alive in all our affairs it cannot be avoided, but it is very subjectively realised. Rather, this is a meditation by a practitioner, one who writes and has written so many radio plays that it is one of the mainstreams of a working life.

Being a radio dramatist alongside a theatre playwright and novelist came naturally and has stayed that way. Why I took to it so quickly, managed to keep it in balance with other work, and still find real pleasure and potential in the form should emerge in what I've put down.

For the sake of having a useful context, it's worth contemplating, that there have been more original plays written for radio in this country over the last eighty years than for the stage over the last four hundred years. Between thirty and forty thousand radio plays have been heard in the houses of the British people, many of them by great writing names, but sound theatre would not have survived and flourished beyond the television onslaught of the Fifties and the rise of commercial radio without the determination of the policymakers of the BBC to keep it alive.

To appreciate the sheer volume and diversity of this great stream of work requires a special kind of consideration today. Radio theatre does not receive the critical attention it did ten years ago, as if it has somehow been incorporated into a background domestic soundscape – which may be a strength. However, in spite of this neglect, it flows on, and will continue to do so. As far as the future is concerned, it can only get stronger. There are many places for it yet to go. No other form of theatre is so well equipped to penetrate the deep, narrow places of human experience, probing into any kind of life or inanimacy a playwright chooses to invest with the power of language.

I hope my love of the form presents itself so evidently it needs no further mention. How it came to pass that Oberon saw fit to commission the book might make itself obvious as well. It has made me look back over nearly four decades of writing radio plays, in the glory days sometimes as many as six in a year. Renewing the connection with the mind that wrote them, and reliving relationships with a dozen and a half different directors, scores of actors, famous and journeymen, and production-team experts, alive and dead, has been, strangely enough, a rejuvenating experience. The deeper I dug down into what radio drama has meant to me, what I've got out of it and what it's got out of me, the more solid and optimistic the future of the form appeared to be.

So, this is no requiem. I believe radio plays are not only here to stay, but will develop even more importance as English grows in strength and brilliance to become the first global language, aided by swiftly advancing technology.

* * *

Accusations of elitism are hurled at those who have taken seriously what they were taught in terms of getting all they can out of the arts for the sake of a better life. This has been going on for forty years. Education in the arts from childhood to the early twenties should not only improve our civilisation but also provide pleasures that greatly improve life. The values of the mass audience are not necessarily those of people who have responded to the arts. Tastes created by popular commercial forces have been in the ascendant since the end of World War II. Because the arts have occupied them heart and soul, some people need the arts as much as others need popular entertainment.

* * *

Chapter IV

THERE ARE SEVEN radios in this house. If alone when listening to another playwright's work that sounds promising, I turn all seven on and go from room to room at normal walking pace, covering three miles during an hour-long broadcast, not missing a word. If this appears odd behaviour all I can say is it comes from an inner sense that radio theatre and exercise go together. The derogation, *couch potato*, is never applied to radio listeners.

Last night, from eight-forty-five to ten-thirty I listened to Webster's *The White Devil* in bed, heard every word clear as a bell. Tangentially, on the national news at six-thirty this morning there was a debate over whether it was reasonable to ask an A-level examinee if Hamlet wanted to avenge his mother rather than his father. There will be an episode of a five-part play on *Woman's Hour* later this morning, and a forty-five minute new play at two-fifteen this afternoon. This is a sample of what is available, our everyday wealth of opportunity to listen to invisible theatre, to take a chance of being entertained, appalled, enlightened or disappointed.

We listen a lot in this country. It is a strong element in our national life, the way we are, the way we live, an important part of our cultural surroundings, a strand in the weave of our civilisation.

Short on sunlight, lacking brilliance in the air, we are an enclouded people of the ear rather than the eye. Our best-known national characteristic, British reserve, has always been misunderstood. We are simply folk whose natural inclination is not to talk, but to listen.

* * *

Aristotle's view that the stage gives even an amoral story authority, does not apply to any of the technical variants of theatre. There is a quality in a live actor up there in front of you remembering lines and moves that goes straight to the deepest recess of human sympathy. If the performance is blown, it is catastrophically embarrassing: if it is magnificent, we are transported. There are half-measures, indifferent performances, lots of them, but there is always a deeper mystery at work in our compassion for the stage. We know something can go wrong. There is a primary risk. Try as we may in radio, film or television, we cannot lead any audience by the nose to the point where that empowering compassion appears because all the risk is secondary – whether the piece will be acceptable or not.

* * *

CHAPTER IV

If theatre is an actor remembering his lines stuck out in front of a live audience, and film and television rely on an actor caught in a camera taking lines off autocue, radio drama is an actor making vocal love to a microphone while turning the pages of the script with exquisite care so as not to make unwanted sound. If we value delicacy, precision and purity, the actor in the radio studio is your man. Fastidiousness is everything.

The playwright's word is kept, not workshopped out of the window, or cut to ribbons in the editing. At a certain level we still have our old status outside the machine.

Watching television together has become the central image of family life today. It's what is left after the disintegration of fellowship within the home produced by computer ownership. Once it was the family gathered round listening to the radio that tugged at the heart. During the war this scene had much warmth and symbolism because this was how great events arrived in the minds of ordinary people. Before the advent of radio people could only read about these things in the newspaper, later they heard it from the new BBC, now they see the whole political scene of the world in a glut of seeing. Being born into listening times, these were hefty collisions for my childish mind, reeling from the impression of being born into a madhouse that was the world at war. All the horrors, defeats, descents into hell and victories emanated from that little brown bakelite wireless to the right of the fire, wreathed in my grandfather's cigarette smoke.

To that generation of children sound still has an atavistic ascendancy, a personal emphasis in folk memory that is a hangover from those war years. When I observed that my grandmother from 1953 onwards stopped reading four romantic novels from the library a week and listening to the radio, preferring to watch television instead, I knew the world had changed. Though I concede no radio report or play could convey the full horror of the Nazi death camps, and lines were drawn for the BBC correspondents because mere words crumbled, yet there was a darkening of the voice, a mysterious mood that said: we've never been here before. We cannot believe this. It was beyond the means of language but not the means of sound. What wasn't said was more important than what was – and that had a sound of its own.

* * *

It all started with sound. Before it was a vibratory event, the Big Bang was a thought. Let's say it was an explosive thought in the mind of the creative power when it was fuming irascibly on a wavelength.

Another view of these origins, a bit closer to tradition, is contained in a radio play I wrote in 2000 about the biography of the English sentence, *I Want To Go Home*, directed by Peter Kavanagh.

CARK: *(who is a glottal)* And on the seventh day God ended his work and rested, going over in his mind the list of what he'd made.

GOD: Light and dark. Seas and dry land. Plants and herbs. Fish and fowl. Creeping things. Mankind. Hmm. It's very quiet down there.

CARK: And on the eighth day God had to go back to work because he'd left something out.

GOD: Let there be sound. Let there be noise.

MEDLEY OF CRASHES, POPS, POURINGS

GOD: Let there be language.

WILD HYSTERICAL JABBERING

In the scheme of things sound accompanies release or withdrawal of energy. Pythagoras, while trying to define the nature of music, found a mathematical pattern in the relationship between sound and materials. He believed the stars made music – and so they must, as our world does with its winds and waves and eruptions passing through the minds of composers.

However, music passes the intellect by. If Pythagoras had extended his experiment with vibrating strings to study the difference between the sung and the unsung word what would have emerged? The sung word divides at the frontier of the mind – sense goes one way, musical sound another. The unsung word goes on alone. This must have something to do with detectable vibrations. If one turns on the radio and a person is speaking, why is it immediately obvious whether someone is acting or not? It is not merely pitch. The sensitivity of our response to the human voice shaped by art is extraordinarily acute.

Are there any other dimensions to dialogue? When we hear characters screaming and roaring at each other in a radio play the hand goes towards the volume control. For dramatic effect that uses only sound, nuances in a flow of *conversation* propel the movement of the action. An unholy row is best conducted in intense whispers. Sex – well, all we've got is heavy breathing before we're in to talking-dirty phone services.

* * *

If we can hear actors but not see them and there is a dramatic form to what is being said, then the territory of the mind that responds to ritual has been entered. No matter how familiar we become with radio theatre it continues to occupy this area, wearing the mask of invisibility. If we listen to the same drama of voices on a daily basis, and the priesthood of actors is the same, as in soap opera, the more ritualised we become.

* * *

Not that it's a choice that needs trouble people, but whether to be deaf is worse than to be blind is a question for a quiet corner on a rainy day in anyone's meditative life.

Sound can matter more than sight. It betrays us less. It has no treacherous dancing surfaces. We have to listen carefully to understand, and while we listen we are measuring, exercising judgement.

Guesswork is good on radio. Working things out in the head is good on radio. Not being cheated or hoodwinked or seduced are good on radio. Arguments are put under close scrutiny. What people think, then say, then do, is at the heart of a radio play – indeed, it is a main strength of the medium – and the crucial gaps between thinking, saying and doing can be sharply represented. As we go further through those gaps, we find more levels of complexity. Conscious thought deepens until it touches instinct – something else radio can be good at – but without resorting to incoherence.

Film dialogue is now so incoherent and slapdash, the skipping over plot narratives, not tying up loose ends so persistent, that the art of movie-making is taking its leave of language except as audial brushwork to touch up images. Because radio plays rely on dialogue and consistent, followable plot for ninety-five per cent of their effect – and therein resides the beating heart of the medium – it is as if the maintenance of clear, strong, vivid use of dramatic language in the technical arts has devolved onto the radio playwright.

If we lose track of the thought in a radio play, the action collapses – whereas in film, this failing can be covered over with sights to amuse the eye. Anything haphazard endangers the wholeness of what we hear but the eye seeks variety to the point of chaos. A crude jump-cut in sound remains a sore point in the mind of the listener, whereas the viewer forgives and forgets the brutality without thinking about it. We learn less from what we see on the screen than what we hear on the radio because the eye craves surfaces, not centres.

Sound has high standards – integrity and purity are inherent because the visible world has to be created within two imaginations – the playwright's and the listener's. Proofs from outside the mind don't work. No radio play should appeal to the eye for its effect. All verbs of seeing should be kept out of the dialogue. Every sight can be conveyed by using the other senses.

The radio play is not yet a hundred years old – hardly out of its infancy. The deep well of the mind has not yet run dry. If the day arrives when high-intelligence computers rule the world and human leisure-time is infinite, the radio play may be part of what keeps us sane. It retains a sense of youth bound to a feeling for history. Like a child living under too much educational control, it struggles with its masters.

* * *

CHAPTER IV

It's twelve years ago and I'm in a motel room in Memphis, Tennessee, watching Sunday morning god-slot television – which is how the great majority of Christians go to church in those parts. An advertisement appears for a buy-two-get-a-third-one-free offer on Bible story videos, including the miracle from the ninth chapter of Mark's gospel where Jesus drives out an evil spirit. The special effect of the evil spirit emerging from the man's mouth as a wraith of smoke, like a genii coming out of a lamp, is oddly disturbing, reminiscent to me of smoking cigars, an abandoned passion. Admiring the technical wizardry, in awe of the titanic commercialism behind it, I hear the gospel text running on the soundtrack beneath, and am reminded of what particular kind of evil spirit it was that was being cast out – one that made its victim foam and gnash in the bitterest of all frustrations, that of being deaf and dumb.

The rest of the day was taken up with a long car journey. The power of the visual trick in the video kept nagging away. How would you get that moment over on radio? What would that evil spirit *sound* like? I sketched a radio version of the miracle while driving along. A radio Christ bringing an isolated soul out of the torture of silence – *I charge thee, come out of him, and enter no more into him.* What would that have to sound like? Thunder? Hiroshima? What voice would Jesus have? Brian Blessed?

Bringing the world's ancient religions to book, presenting their heavens and hells in all their lurid, crazed magnificence, is rare. The 2009 BBC reading of the whole of Milton's *Paradise Lost* with Anton Lesser is the nearest I've heard.

In radio the listener is incorporated into the action, let into the secret. There is a contribution of self to be made. If I didn't know that Shakespeare wrote *Henry V* for the stage, I'd swear that Chorus is referring to radio here:

For 'tis your thoughts that now must deck our kings
Carry them here and there; jumping o'er times,
Turning the accomplishment of many years
Into an hour-glass:

* * *

The biggest rumpus ever caused by a radio play was in the United States.

Orson Welles produced H.G. Wells' *War of the Worlds* in 1938 with his Mercury Theatre and caused panic when people listening believed aliens were actually invading the Earth. This panic has recently been put into doubt. The allegation is that Welles cooked it up as a publicity stunt. Even a report by a known newsreader in a play is detectable as a part of the fiction. You cannot make drama sound like authentic real life. It always has the edge of artifice, for which we should be grateful. The human ear refuses to let go of its supersensitivity to the distinction.

* * *

When an art form is created by inventive technology (the theatre of radio, film and television), as the technology improves the new art form may be expected to improve along with it, advancing at a similar pace, making use of developments.

The technologies behind film and television have swept upwards alongside computer science, but the arts made out of them have been left to languish far behind. In the case of radio, the improvements in the technology are there, but they hardly relate to drama. The single room studio with one microphone is still at the heart of it all. No amount of computerised sound control advances has changed the essential elements. In many ways, the art of radio theatre is as robust as its beginnings, and still shows the signs of its origins.

* * *

While its death on television is annually mourned and moidered over at the Mediaguardian Edinburgh television festival, the single play is alive and kicking on BBC Radio. A single play is a drama on its own, unlinked – not a serial, not a series. It has an individual shape and depth of structure recognisable as a theatre form in origin. The reason it has survived on radio is that the cultural roots of the form go deeper than television, and fashion and finance hurricanes have not brought it down. When drama is mentioned at the Mediaguardian festival, it doesn't mean what a playwright means by drama. In the parlance of today's television, drama is the new breed of film, in series, drawn from what purports to be public taste and crisis consciousness: terrorism, security, police, detection, and spies.

What people watch as drama on-screen is expected to be more lightweight, more violent, more highly coloured, more irrational than what they hear. The rules are different. The eye asks fewer questions and demands more playthings. The ear loves subtlety of argument, shifts of emphasis, and – most of all – people trying to talk their way dynamically out of situations, or into their obsessions.

There are new single plays being produced in the theatre, but in wildly varied production environments. The difference between the stages of the National Theatre and pub back rooms is such that a playwright has trouble straddling the gulf between. In the theatre of sound this separation is not a problem.

All new radio plays have the same backing, the BBC, and the same invisible stage, the mind of the public. The mind for radio is judged to be different to the mind for television. The BBC for radio, and the BBC for television, are two very different entities with mindsets facing in separate directions. One chases the audience, the other protects it.

Each year there are five hundred or so new pieces broadcast by the BBC. Some of them are sold on to other countries. British radio theatre is the liveliest, most productive in the world. To quibble that the quality of the plays is uneven is to state the obvious. How can five hundred radio plays all reach the same level of achievement? If they did it would be an ominous sign that we were bumping along the bottom, and commerce of some kind had made a conquest.

* * *

Radio theatre is not the sovereign territory of a technology. It is the open field of the emotions, the vaults of memory.

The recorded voice bears the imprint of its time, the accents of great wars, of social struggle, of difference, of class, of nationality, of mood and temper. We listen to those hieratic voices from the Thirties brittle and charged with priestly superiority. In a way it is as much folk music as the agricultural labourer's harvest song. History is there in the tone, the way people speak, the attitudes. Open the radio playwright's black drawer and these ghosts of the air are set free. The dead speak again, the wars are re-fought and all the burning questions lie there recoverable.

* * *

What a playwright produces for radio is closer to the generative sources of the mind, and freer of contraptions, than all other types of literature, including poetry. The stage playwright is burdened with sets, the novelist with paragraphs of interiors and landscapes, the film scriptwriter with cameras, the poet with rhyme, scansion and form, and being aware of his own voice above others.

Dialogue being the main business of radio theatre keeps the trappings of soundscapes to a minimum, though the aural atmosphere is a highly sensitive area. An atmosphere that is wrong can be very annoying to the listener. There are directors with supersensitive talents in this area. Listening to their work in the control room during a recording my hearing can't keep up sometimes. They hear beyond my range like bats.

It is possible to produce all the sound effects for a play through the mouths of actors. There was a piece on Radio 4 recently set in a Russian travelling circus where an actor barked like a dog throughout a long scene. It was obviously a human imitation, a dialogue dog saying something. That worked very well in a circus play where animals were taught to do tricks, including the human animal.

A proposal to the BBC commissioning editor that I've had my name on for some time, is for an adaptation of George Orwell's *Animal Farm* with the actors not only playing the spoken parts of the anthropomorphicized animals but also providing all the background farmyard sounds – clucking, grunting, mooing, neighing, plus tractors, cars, milking-machines, shotguns etc. That way the sound effects will be integrated with the human sound to a much greater extent and George Orwell's satire on state Communism made sharper and more poignant.

* * *

Mental adventure is the meat and drink of radio plays. Its friends and allies are intensity, quietness, softness, steeliness, warmth, civil snottiness, inward exploration and music – its enemies are the shout, the scream, loudness of all kinds, gabbling, the gun in my right hand is loaded, look over yonder there's a house on fire, chaos and incoherence.

Of all the technical forms of theatre, it is still only half out of the box it was bought in. It has the capacity, largely untapped, to accurately present difficult moods of twentieth-century thought, that strange, inchoatively heartbreaking mixture of nihilism, existentialism, fatalism and the absurd.

* * *

So, what level of artistic achievement can sound theatre rise to? How far up the scale of dramatic fulfillment can it go? Can it ever compete with the great unforgetable moments the stage provides? Where, when it is being most successfully realised, does it stand in the conflict between sentiment and sense?

There are limitations beyond those already marked out. Without an audience in a pack the highest catharsis is impossible. It is as if the collective soul only works at its most intense register when people are physically bound by the same space. At some point all the different experiences people are having while watching a stage play can coalesce into one superb sensation everyone shares. Any stage playwright looks back on those moments – if lucky enough – with more than satisfaction – the night it all worked, when the play, the actors and the audience fused into a manifestation of what was originally intended, plus the social creativity of director and actors. Being as complex and intricate a business as it is to put a play on the stage, one cannot talk about perfection, only a force that pushes a performance beyond the province of that judgement. But this is a social ecstasy, not an individual response. The height of spiritual uplift it can attain far outstrips anything that radio, or film or television can ever achieve.

To be fortunate enough to number the times it happens in your own work on the fingers of one hand would be a great blessing indeed – in a lifetime of theatre-going, well, if you can count twenty that's reason to be grateful.

This argues for radio theatre seeking its own inimitable excellence where it cannot be challenged or put into the shade. Because of its history of controls and the vulgarisation of managements seeking wider audiences, it has never been allowed to incline towards its own special aesthetic. What experiments have been made tended to be based on tabu subjects rather than creating a new listening experience. When the argument is made that radio theatre is a medium of experiment for writers it generally means there is another form that will benefit – a proposed novel, film or stage play. No one has used the radio more in this capacity than I have. The flexibility and interchangeability of ideas between a play on the radio and the same story in a separate existence acts as strengthening of plot and character.

* * *

In 2050 anyone who served in the armed forces during World War II will definitely be dead. This is surely the moment to bring Remembrance Day to an end, or extend it to embrace the fallen in every war our people have ever fought in – against Romans, Anglo-Saxons, Vikings, Normans, both sides in the Civil War, French, Dutch, Spanish, French, Indians, Russians, native and colonial Americans and Canadians, Zulus, Afghanistanis, Boers, Austrians, Italians, Germans, Turks, and Japanese, to name a few of the enemies we've had, and, in many cases, as is our way, absorbed into the gene pool that is *us,* and the new us then finds new enemies, and they will always have to be absorbed in their turn. The idea of tampering with Remembrance Day would be put forward in cabinet by a courageous minister who knows he hasn't long to live. A radio playwright could make this what-if plot work, and be as certain of a response as someone kicking a sacred cow at a holy festival.

* * *

It is a dangerous thing for playwrights to want people to think well of them. Often they put a great deal of effort into bringing about the opposite result. Some of those who have succeeded most in the theatre have had to pass through a pain barrier of public hostility before discerning critics put the average theatregoer right, telling them what to appreciate. In spite of the very mixed calibre of theatre critics over the last thirty years, that suffering remains a noble one because it means the theatre is exercising its ancient role of being both within and beyond convention, responding to the hunger for renewable artistic truth.

Radio theatre lacks the immense depth of two thousand five hundred years of stage history, but after ninety years it should have developed something that is peculiarly its own. This is no history essay (no one writes a history of what they love – if they do it's proof they don't love it any more) but it's hard not to record how all study of sound theatre in this country inevitably goes back to Dylan Thomas's *Under Milk Wood* (1954), a marvellous piece of radical invention that can be seen, in spite of its poetry, as the prototype for *The Archers.*

There is a sense that it was decided there and then that *Under Milk Wood* was the apogee of the radio play. It had scaled the heights only thirty years after the art form came into being and could only be imitated in a baser formula where the average ruled, as the BBC mandarins declared it must back in the 1920's, but without the poetry that had lifted Thomas's play onto another plane. There is a parallel to the public death of Dennis Potter and the general consensus that he was the last television playwright. From that point on there were only scriptwriters and serials, not playwrights and plays. This is the culture of management despair – the closing down of the future, the destruction of a living art form by design, which is a pretty special kind of wickedness we need to avoid.

The fulfillment of sound theatre's potential will not be found in soap operas, classic serials or urban everyday melodramas. There are plays still to be written with delving thought energies, psychological patterns and shifts of character that will astound the ear and lead to fresh enlightenment.

* * *

Chapter V

A COLD, WET SPRING evening, nineteen seventy-two. A mobile theatre, the Century, stands jacked up in a car park in the middle of Preston. It's ten-thirty. The audience is coming out of a farce, my first professionally produced piece of theatre in the United Kingdom. The plot is the template (so I claim) for every film, novel and play that's based on the idea of growing cannabis commercially – this time in a failing north-country garden centre. There is a nun, an amateur terrorist, a big, tough left-wing mother, a close harmony group of weirdos called *The Smoke Cats* and others. I'm waiting outside the foyer to catch what people thought as they passed on their way home, a cold wind is blowing – and this lot didn't think much of the play anyhow.

A man with a smile and a twinkle joins me in the dark place where I've chosen to snoop. 'My name's Alfred Bradley," he says. 'I work for the BBC. How would you like to write a play for radio?'

Here was a man who'd sought me out to put an idea in my head. (I noticed he didn't ask me to adapt the play he'd seen). Writers enjoy that kind of thing. It makes them believe they might be doing something to contradict what Emile Zola said about authorship:

In the nothing of everything writing remains
the most enthralling of all useless enterprises.

* * *

On December 2nd 1972, the day this inaugural play was broadcast – *Free Ferry*, a half-hour piece in a series called *Four Morning Plays,* it shared a page in *Radio Times* with *Listen With Mother*, *The Reith Lectures*, a serial adaptation of a Balzac novel, *The Archers, My Kind of Music* and *The World Tonight* – thirty minutes in the sixteen and three-quarter hours of an entire day's output by Radio 4 from 6.30 am to 11.15 pm.

I remember looking at the page with disconcertment, suffering a few very odd feelings.

Writing a novel, short stories and stage plays had not put me in this position before. To be served up between *The Daily Service* and *You and Yours* was not an enjoyable sensation. What about those people who have the radio on all day? What about those people who have both the radio *and television* on all day? As they go round their houses with the vacuum cleaner can they be said to be listening hard enough to follow a play?

Also I knew that there probably wasn't a single instance of builders at work anywhere throughout Great Britain listening to radio plays on the tranny.

Whatever the problems of having a stage play presented in a mobile theatre built of WWII army surplus vehicles standing in a car park in Preston, the piece was the whole offering for that night, not one item on a very long menu. But a full house in the Century was only two hundred and twenty-five people. The Radio 4 audience at 11.30 am, when *Free Ferry* went out, could be a million. Yet because it was invisible, it seemed smaller, and less trustworthy.

And there was no response *at all*. That was the killer.

It was only a live experience in the studio in Manchester where it was recorded – otherwise nothing. The play fell into a bottomless abyss.

Listening to it at home on the day of transmission had no fellowship. It could not compare with being in a theatre audience, even if they weren't having a great time. Even the non-event of publication day of a novel was better because at least there was the book in your hand, something solid you had made.

The radio experience was nothing.

To take all this in required self-examination followed by spiritual adjustment.

* * *

The crunch came when I was asked to write another piece of radio drama, this time for an hour slot.

Did I want to go through this strange nihilism again if I didn't understand its meaning? There was the money to be considered, but that, though useful, was not substantial for a beginner, calculated on a personal rate per minute that increases the more you do. No reviews of the first play had come out, adding to the odd feeling that nothing had happened. Having got used to the pains and pleasures of public and paper criticism by being published and having a play on stage for a year meant the deficiency was felt. What I had encountered, of course, was the silence – silence that had to be made creative. Writing for the theatre and writing books hadn't put this reality in the frame. Also, I had to confess that in order to deal with criticism I'd developed a deflective apparatus. Did I really need to find out what one or two people thought of my work?

I make no excuse for having these existential thoughts (a trick writers need to have up the sleeve). To be *broadcast*, that is to be a seed widely sown, and to be doomed to fall not even on stony ground but into the Void, may bear thinking about, but there's no need to let it become a point of oppression.

After a very long, thoughtful walk over the moors, I accepted the second commission.

This was the necessary task: write this play knowing what you now know. Handle it intelligently. Most of all – write it for yourself.

When the seed flies out of the basket into nowhere, let the sower be yourself, not the BBC. Never blame the corporation or the public, even when they deserve it. Never be afraid of the great nothing out there because it is only people en masse in disguise.

The subject of *Free Ferry* was a mechanism – the cable ferry acoss Lake Windermere near Bowness. For the second play, *Free House,* it was the Wagon and Horses on the Lune quayside at Lancaster run by an ex-steeplechase jockey who was a genius. When the pub flooded one spring tide and barrels came bobbing through the cellar doors, he carried on serving customers who were already up to their knees in water. When a stage carpenter who had been on a bender came into the pub in his pyjamas, his pint was pulled without comment or question. Les had an *attitude*, but only a play could examine its complexity. No psychiatrist could get near such a man. His wife would see to that.

Although I knew the man who ran the ferry, and the publican, I never told them a play was on – abjuring that base and risky form of flattery. As it was, they both found out from other sources (inhabitants of the Void, obviously) but were very relaxed about it.

I only saw my grandmother in tears on one occasion. Here was a woman who had plenty to cry about, married to a man who was drunk every day. She helped bring me up and I was acutely aware of how she felt, though her life was not one of moods. Comedy, stoicism, a housewife's pride, amazing loyalty were her touchstones. Her tears were shed in 1949 over the death of the Liverpool comedian, Tommy Handley, of wartime ITMA fame. He died of a brain haemorrhage, bending over to pick up a collar stud. Those irreverent half-hour radio shows were cockeyed little plays, shying satirical brickbats at the military and government – all this at the time of the country's greatest peril. Colonel Chinstrap, who was always drunk, had special meaning for her.

As I wrote more radio plays, this matrix of listening history was drawn upon. Often, after a day's work on a text, I would conjure up two memories: one of my grandmother weeping over Tommy Handley; the other her saying goodnight to the BBC presenter who brought television to a close each night. He'd say goodnight, she'd say goodnight, then murmur: 'I do admire that man.'

He was that real, he was that handsome, but when he died I noticed she didn't cry.

* * *

During the time I first wrote plays for radio I was the resident dramatist at the new Duke's Playhouse in Lancaster. Whether what I'm about to relate was coincidence or not, I can't say, but my mind does not have compartments – it would be useful sometimes if it had.

Late-night shows in the studio theatre were popular – more popular than plays on the main stage at that time, it has to be said. Rehearsals were due to start on a sketch I'd adapted from a local folk story called *The Cockey Moor Snake* and I was making my way down the service corridor to the studio when I heard close-harmony singing that was so beautiful it made me stop dead.

It was the northern folk song, *The Unquiet Grave,* being sung by Stephen Boxer, Fiona Victory and Harriet Walter – young multi-talented actors in the Theatre in Education company rehearsing for the late-night show. Although I looked upon myself as musical, if uninformed and under-educated in that field, no other piece I'd ever heard had affected me so much.

From this moment on I thought in terms of what theatre and music could be brought together on stage, and radio. Without those actors and their voices and instruments, the conjunction would never have been made so completely. All the work I subsequently did at Lancaster had a strong musical connection, until the actors left – but then we formed Paines Plough, a new play national touring company that's still going strong thirty-five years on, and Stephen, Fiona and Harriet and other multi-talented actors who had worked at the Duke's returned to do plays similarly based on their skills – all of which were adapted for radio: *Music To Murder By, Richard ll Part Two, Motocar*, and *Beef.* On top of these has to be added *Master Class*, originally written for Paines Plough but first produced at Leicester Haymarket, and a succession of radio plays about composers and musicians; *Satchelmouth,*

Cadenza, Brahms on a Slow Train, Façade, Cuban Solo, Pound on Mr Greenhill and *An Insular Motet.*

* * *

The deeper earth of family life, with all the stones and weeds of childhood, is there to be turned over by the radio playwright's plough. An eighth of all the plays I've written are fictions autobiographically based on those times. It could be some kind of aural eccentricity, but I hear memories before I see them. My mother's voice calling me enters many different sounds. The real source of the sound I know – a bird, perhaps – but there is a sound within a sound. Out of this intensely private world emerges drama akin to many other lives on the surface, but no relationship is the same as another, whether it be between people, or people and ideas, or people struggling with place or time. In spite of appearances, there is little common ground in the way individuals feel and think about life. What seems trite and quotidian to the observer reflects on the tiredness of his mind, not the essence of what is being experienced. All generalisations about human behaviour are based on the false premise that the science behind the organism rules. Uniqueness is the base camp of the lonelines and exposure inherent in each personality. It is also the strength and saving grace to be found at the top of the mountain.

Now you might think this is all being taken far too seriously, but if you ran together all the radio plays I've written over the last thirty-eight years in a listening marathon it would be three and a half days long.

As a companion to go with this awe-inspiring statistic, here's a gnomic notebook extract for a day in March 2009 directly after recording a play in Brighton: *Be thankful for the fool within. If he resigns, your writing arm will soon be in a sling.*

* * *

Voices in the head can be a blessing or a curse, a revelation or a torment; a symptom of mental disorder; a proof of God in the minds of fire-brained prophets; a justification for murder; and a fascinating means of livelihood for playwrights especially sensitive to sound. This often goes with a love of music.

Authors who cannot handle the discipline of sound only, may also suffer these intrusive voices. What is orated in the back of their brains is transferred to the page or the stage, or the screen. But apart from a brief existence in a playscript tossed into a cosmic dustbin, what the voices say in the head of a playwright writing for radio ends up where it started – in the head, and, finally, in the black drawer where the cassettes and CD's of many years of writing sound theatre are kept.

So there's a sense of being dominated by those voices, of always going back to the original experience, the disembodied words in the head, the strange call from over the hill, living in a landscape that hums with human speech, the sound that carries mankind's greatest beauty and spiritual strength in an intensity of thought, feeling, and imaginative life – all in the head where everything important happens.

Sound is as much a spirit world as any myth or fable. Oracles spoke wisdom out of invisibility. That was their magic. The unseen god chose speech because words create belief more than apparition. Hence religions are founded on books, not hallucinations.

* * *

Intermittently, in odd and uneven phases, radio theatre has been my best means of steadying up and asking the questions: what is it you're writing about within yourself? Cleared of the money and the mortal mess, what has been there to be found? Have there been any revelations muscling in from outside your own imagination? If you think there were, can you say they were sent only to you? Is there any way that you represent the age you have written through, and for? In a hundred years time, if someone encounters your work while browsing the 2110 Wondernet, is it remotely possible it will mean anything at all?

As time passes answers to these questions become more important, more necessary, because age enhances the danger of losing one's way through lack and excess of self-criticism, and wasting time spinning through spirals of guilt. Much has been written in order to live and raise a family and be like anyone else. The energy and ambition to rise above this will not last for ever but the inner ear can remain cocked, and the mind remain strong and capable of craft and balance. There is a pattern in what has been written, a pattern to be completed, a final unity of being still findable, but it's a complex one, not created by the rules of any kind of cultural geometry, or expectation generated in hopeful youth. To want to hear one's own voice speaking clearly through the trained and talented voices of others is, if they are assembled against the silence one understands, nothing to do with Narcissus, everything to do with making sense of it all.

* * *

What kind of story is it that arrives stamped *radio play*? It can be an adventurous plot that scorns all physical limitations, but as we know and understand the traditions of radio drama and the way it is usually written, there are strange intellectual restrictions. The great majority of radio plays are set in the domestic box, as were the early television plays. Although radio can realise any piece of theatre or novel or short story, stepping over the bounds of any other form, at home in the outer and inner mind, there is a strong element of conservatism at work. Writers with a high degree of idiosyncratic style find it difficult to get a start in writing plays for radio. If they get past the door of the BBC, they tend to be wheeled into the recording of a domestic soap opera as an observer to learn the ropes.

Each country respects the sources of its language, and its guardians of the word. Ours have been rooted in broadcasting for the last eighty years. Radio remains truer to the pioneer principles of the BBC than television, because it was the original and only voice. The conservatism starts here.

If a piece of apparatus can be called natural, radio is natural to the human organism. When a radio play goes out it is *on the air,* being breathed. When a play of mine is transmitted I sit down and listen with the invisible people, imagining the audience – even though I've had the CD of the recording for months. It is the only time there is contact, vast, faceless but oddly intense like very high atmospheric pressure. I don't imagine people in sitting rooms, I sense minds on a horizon – a horizon where there is no applause, only the absorbency of space.

Sometimes there are phone calls, letters and e-mails after a play is transmitted but response is fragmentary, desultory and often one hears the screech of the unhinged. There's no point aching for the buzz of a theatre audience. Your play has been put into orbit. It has no time to get rusty and become junk.

Within a very short time it disintegrates, then disappears. It can have an existence in the British Library Sound Archive, like a mummy in a pyramid.

In order to be ready to write another one, and give it all you've got, you need either to be hardened to this disheartening evaporation, or discover it has virtues.

* * *

To illustrate the variety of mind the radio playwright might encounter, and has to be braced for, here is a quote from the BBC Listeners Log for April 14th, 2000, the only phoned-in responses to one of my plays:

Mrs Ruth Rees – This is the the most boring play I have ever listened to.

Miss P Marshall – Thought it was marvellous.

* * *

Writing minds divide up into streams. Theatre, radio drama, the novel, dance theatre, opera, poetry flow separately over the delta, touching, combining, separating again. The author may be carried along by a single stream at a time, but the sense of one river remains.

* * *

What are the essential requirements for a commercially successful film?

As detailed in the movie, *Sweet Liberty*, they are: disrespect for authority, destruction of property and the removal of clothes.

No such list can be made for the radio play.

Besides, the idea of a commercially successful radio play has not been around for a long time. But, for the sake of argument, what might those ingredients be, using the *Sweet Liberty* formula as a guide? There's not a lot to be said for the removal of clothes; sound effects on CD of the destruction of property are available, much employed in Blitz reminiscences, but they are hardly a big attraction for the listener; as for disrespect for authority…well, on radio that tends to be teenage stuff in a mature aural medium.

I have heard writerly mutterings about illness in children, drugs in Manchester, and infidelity in Islington, but choose to believe such flip judgements indicate there are no templates for the ear.

* * *

A radio play is recorded in a room with one glass wall – a space cut off from the world. If there are no people in this room, the studio is standing idle, and the silence is complete. If for any reason you intrude upon that – being the first to arrive for a day of recording, for instance – the silence you encounter has a density greater than that of a mausoleum at midnight, yet it is also enlivened and pregnant. The silence will always be there, even when other people have arrived and fill the space with chatter. The silence is held in the head. The silence outside and inside the head is the mentor of everything said in radio theatre.

A red light warns anyone outside the studio not to enter. Although it says *recording in progress*, what it means is *respect the silence we are breaking.* If you go to a sacred grove anywhere expect to encounter the same.

The B10 studio in the basement of Broadcasting House was subject to the rumble of underground Victoria Line trains going in and out of Oxford Street station. If a train went past, work in the studio stopped. The scripts went down. The background silence that the actors were working with was removed.

That silence was a part of the play when the playwright started the script, trusting that only the sounds he asks for will be heard in the finished piece. The silence was the first thing he encountered in his mind when he sat down to write. It is not the enemy, as the blank page is to the novelist. Silence is a power much greater than the blank page because it is the infrastructure of the sound. It is the unsung note and the uncreated thought. Behind every word, every sound effect, every atmosphere, will be the silence. The blank page will disappear under the written word but the silence never will.

Never put a pause at the end of a speech in a radio play because silence is volatile in its power, reaching out immediately to grab sense and push it aside. Put the pause in the middle of the speech where it can be part of the thought. As the Egyptian desert hermits knew from their imagined conversations with the divine (very early radio model here), silence is the friend of creative thought.

* * *

A composer is coming here to talk about a project we've had on the stocks for twenty years – the adaptation of a stage play into a chamber opera. There's some interest from a Sicilian company. Perhaps the composer could get a commission. The story might attract them because the setting is sixteenth-century Italy, the Kingdom of the Two Sicilies. There's a need to get reacquainted with the text and be clear how the piece works. In the black drawer is a cassette of a BBC radio adaptation recorded in 1976 with the original cast. All that needs to be done is put it on the tape deck and listen.

As the black drawer is opened, awe enters the equation.

The lead was played by an actress once very close who died five years ago.

Better to say *is played,* actually, because she'll be there.

By virtue of her everlastingly live voice caught on magnetic tape, she'll be in the room.

Her picture on the wall is a dead thing in comparison. It doesn't mean she's in the room. A picture is mere image with no depth, a one-dimensional thing. The sound of the human voice has every dimension there is, every power and every beauty. As soon as *play* is pressed and she says the first line, she'll be here, and for ninety minutes.

When she dies in the final scene, that will be a difficulty. She dies twice. Am I strong enough for that? Where does she go? Where does the play go? There'll be an aftermath, a torrent of thought. That is a creative moment – being haunted is something to be valued in a playwright's life.

The extraordinary telling power of the voice was made physically eternal a hundred and twenty years ago by the invention of sound recording. Hear the scratchy wax cylinders of Edison's phonograph from the 1890's – Tennyson in his death-fearing old age choosing to declaim *The Charge of the Light Brigade* as his grand aural monument. (Another radio play here). Imagine the unrecorded host of voices from the past, great floods of medieval sermons that if put end to end would outdo all geological history – it's good to believe that all are vibrating somewhere, craving a new life inside our technical mastery.

Today we exist in a strange loop of sound, forever turning. We love the motion of this loop. It provides security to the modern mind. As long as we stay within it, we'll stay on top, equipped to survive with knowledge of what's going on around us. But issues of natural life and death are carried away into a whirlpool by this loop we live in. Information is sucked down with news, tragedy with indifference, comedy with cruelty. Attempts to analyse this swirling mixture become part of the huge stream of sound. Bobbing along, in danger of being sucked down, is the radio play, needing a moment when the loop stops and the whirlpool ceases in which to be heard to advantage.

As a dramatic form its heyday might be the time when we rescue ourselves from the whirlpool and give our ears a chance, living in a more disciplined, but newly attentive way.

The playwright of the air works on the principle that all truth can be found in sound.

* * *

The greater number of the plays I've written for the stage and radio concern artists – composers, authors, painters and poets, or people with political power. The plays I wrote for television in the Eighties don't fall within this description. They were about ordinary people under stress of some kind, and I was aware of being hustled to write them in a certain way by an industry that looked upon itself as the voice of the people, adopting editorial powers that were far too strong. The advantage of writing plays with characters who have already carved out their place in history is they have pre-existent authority, as Shakespeare knew.

* * *

Having written a stage play (*Getting The Picture)* and a radio play *(Something To Remember You By*) about the heat and cold of photography, the subject obviously fascinates, but whether I've ever managed to get on top of it is another matter. I was first struck by the strangely repellent aspects of image-taking at a Nativity play put on for parents at a nursery school. No one was watching the kids on the stage because the whole audience was videoing the performance – which meant they would never see the real thing. When the video was looked at in later years, perhaps when the children had become parents themselves, the chilling absurdity of the occasion would not be there – only the sentiment.

* * *

The playwright builds a structure using what he trusts is the listener's working knowledge of people in a world forever inclined to outlandishness. No matter how absurd or cruel or generous or self-sacrificing imagined actions are, someone, somewhere has carried them out. No radio playwright spends time explaining the obvious to the audience – what they should already know. Behind every play is an assumption that people are aware of what they're living through, can think about it and realise how strange life can be. That is how touchstones work – points of reference the writer can make to common experience, cross references in a medium that is outwardly blind and inwardly all-seeing.

* * *

Choosing good plots solely for the ear is not far away from selecting a topic of conversation you want to have with intellectual superiors. Watch what you say. Think it through before you open your mouth. Make them laugh, by all means, but don't leave yourself wide open by using weak arguments. If forced to be mundane to make a point, rememember the dividing line between theatre and soap opera.

* * *

In the whole of my writing life I've only ever copied down two bits of overheard dialogue, which says something about my observational working methods being based more on starting-points and surmise than record.

The first was heard on an underground train from Liverpool to Birkenhead late on a Friday night in 1966 while sitting behind two Irishmen:

A: What day is it tomorrow?

B: Easter Sunday.

A: When Jesus rose from the dead.

B: You can't keep a good man down.

The second was dialogue overheard in my own dream. In the middle of a vast wheatfield in the steppes of Russia a farmer stands with his pig-tailed blonde daughter beside a beautiful new tractor full of amazing gadgets:

FARMER: Here we are with all the latest technology but you manage to get pregnant in the same old way.

I managed to use the dream dialogue in a dance-play, *The Edge,* written for The Kosh, but the Irishmen remain on their late-night train under the Mersey, forever on their journey, in spite of a long-held thought that there's a radio play in there, somewhere, mystical in character, involving two saints chatting on an underground train that goes beneath the Irish Sea from Liverpool to Dublin with one branch line to Belfast, and another to the Infernal Regions.

* * *

For a country teeming with dialect it is odd that nearly all our radio drama in Britain is heavily weighted towards only a few regions – the north, London Home Counties and estuarine, Edinburgh/Glasgow, Ulster. After all these years dealing with the voices of the British Isles I found myself recently having to ask what a South Lincolnshire accent sounds like.

* * *

A writer's imaginative life has rhythmless surges and declines that appear in notebooks, outbursts of optimism and descents into the pit, often on facing pages. The strangeness of the process never fades, which is a good thing because we never want to get used to it, and if the note-making compulsion weakens, and the oscillations of mood flatten out, you know atrophy could be around the corner.

In fallow times while sifting through these notebooks life-saving ideas can be spotted. Some are in the guise of a chrysalis, dry and unattractive, even in their noteworthiness; others suddenly flare up full of colour and potential for flight. An idea can be passed over many times, rejected because it is either too drab or too gaudy, then suddenly it speaks again with the warmth and force that made it originally worth noting.

Writers are storytellers, reformers, elucidators, imparters, moralisers, observers, and entertainers. All of those who work off a factitious, fictional art base will claim to be the last of these first – entertainers, certainly not scholars, even if their natural working purlieu seems to be intellectual, the creation of good education and wide reading. What elements they will own of the other functions listed is not particularly to be trusted. After the continual media debate and analysis of the arts, the psychological scrutiny and theories, and thousands of hours of interview time with writers, no full explanation has surfaced. The argument that writers wish to recreate the world so they can have the power to manipulate their own version of it is an attractive one – and that this curious instinct stems from disappointment with the world as it is stemming from childhood trauma and loss, is psychologically alluring, and seems to fit many individual cases. Whatever the nature of the authorial psyche, it definitely harbours the urge to make notes on everything that moves. This smacks of empirical science as much as art – the gathering of evidence to prove a theory, or the gathering of information to see if a pattern emerges.

Perhaps science and the arts have always been much closer than we think.

* * *

It might be interesting to look at the life of a play from the original emergence of the idea, through a few complex turns that are not unusual in the making of radio theatre. The one I have chosen came into being via a costly failure in another form, the novel, which didn't work. The story will, hopefully, illustrate the special superiority radio theatre has over other mediums in dealing with difficult ideas, yet retaining dramatic power and how essential clarity of purpose and primacy of dialogue can lift a play out of a hundred-thousand word morass of fiction.

Stolen Time was a ninety-minute play for BBC Radio 4. It was broadcast on 28th February, 1998, directed by Eoin

O'Callaghan. The trigger entry in the 1994 notebook is: *The day after Sept 2nd 1752 became Sept 14th*. On the next page is the mention of Thomas Gray's *Elegy In A Country Churchyard,* that most time-conscious of poems, published in 1751, the year before the calendar change, then a few pages of notes about Gray's friendship with Horace Walpole, the prime minister who expedited the shift from the Julian to the Gregorian calendar.

The novel was preferred for the story, probably because space for disquisition and discursiveness are inherent to the form, but foreign to the theatre. If more than twelve facts are put in a stage play the audience start to suffer.

Nothing is more attractive to an author as an exploration of Time. The abstractness is not only beauty in itself, but a common experience. The public love to have Time made flexible, especially if there are machines involved. Time is also the poet's wound, the priest's right hand, the philosopher's framework. But the deeper you dig, the more reality disappears and mysticism arises – and this executive measure by Walpole was taken for reason of trade with no reference to the supernatural or the god of the established Anglican church. All our European markets were on the Gregorian calendar. Great Britain's dates not being synchronised with trading partners was causing problems.

Three months later, written at breakneck speed, the manuscript of the doomed novel was finished. Its characters and the theme of the lost eleven days as a parallel to real time in which events of the spirit happened were blurred by a welter of metaphysics and descriptions of mountain scenery.

This misfortunate enterprise happened at a point when I could have done without a wasteful failure of this kind. Productive time had been lost, never mind Walpole's eleven days. I had also managed to lose my way with great enthusiasm. The reaction of my supporters: wife, agent, fellow writers, friends, was the same. What I had done was somehow beyond criticism, being rather typical of a trap I fall into. Someone described the novel as having been written for a niche market of horologists. What truly worried me most was my original judgement. What had I thought so noteworthy in the whole business of taking a chunk out of Time? It's something we do as a matter of course as we travel through zones, why we get jet-lagged. Besides, Time is never altered in truth because it doesn't exist in truth, only on paper.

For three years the idea was banished, but it continued to camp on the border of that part of memory where the concerns of livelihood predominate. Then, while recording a play about Ezra Pound, Monteverdi and Ginsberg set in Venice, directed by Eoin O'Callaghan, the subject came up *as a story*. What surprised me was how clear it was in my mind, as if, during the intervening years, a structure had evolved. That night I took out the manuscript of the novel, wondering whether to attempt a complete rewrite. The difference between the prose I was reading and the story I had told at the lunch break was enormous. Before long I realised that I had taken the wrong decision in the first place. It was never a novel. Although it remained a complex and difficult tale, now it was only half so because the ambience of the radio studio, concentrating on a text with actors of the quality of Stephen Boxer and Alun Armstrong, had simplified and synthesised what had been going on in my head for ages.

It had always been a story for the ear. Radio 3 with its rock-hard audience of devotees, ready for anything, was the place for it. By the time the recording with Eoin was over, a radio play on the lost eleven days had emerged in synopsis. In discussions with the BBC no mention was made of the unpublished novel lying in the bottom drawer. It's still there, a useful reminder of the importance of getting early decisions right, and how writing time can be lost, but an idea not wasted.

This is not to say that a good novel could not have been created out of the idea I had come across. Another writer with a firmer grasp on metaphysical tendencies within the self might make a success of it. There may even be a novel already written based on emotional responses to messing about with time, possibly in French. After the Revolution, Napoleon brought in completely new names for the months, for instance – determined to show how much things had changed.

In that case they were all changed back later, proof of the failure and futility of the revolutionary instinct, which makes it even more interesting because things *had* changed, and for ever.

* * *

As a laboratory for research into the operation of dramatic ideas radio has no rival. The enrichening interchange with other forms is extraordinary. After the experience of recording *Stolen Time,* there would have been nothing unusual in turning back to the novel, or making a stage play or film script, or even a poem out of it. The power of dialogue only and the relentless focus on making sense by means of the verbal microscope opens up potential in all directions, liberating both character and motivation, stimulating fresh action.

The cast of hundreds in the failed novel spiralled down to four. Scores of different scenes set in the lost eleven days and the parallel times shrank to one afternoon on a track leading to a fellside cottage where the dénouement takes place. Thomas Gray, the poet of *Elegy in a Country Churchyard*, has gone up into the mountains to escape the political uproar over the change to the calendar. There are riots all over England, protesting against Parliament's high-handedness. People simply do not understand how the day after September 2nd can possibly be September 14th on the mere say-so of politicians.

At the moment the days are lost (including feast days, holidays, birthdays, deathdays) – midnight on September 2nd – Gray intends to be alone on a mountain top, safe with the stars, and in his own proper time, which is based on his relationship with the universe. Gray meets Hudson, a hill farmer who is, in fact, a lord who, along with an offer of patronage, had sent Gray a sheaf of his own efforts at poetry for an opinion and received an honest if cruel reply. The lord intends to exact a special revenge for this insult by killing Gray in the absolute centre of the Void, the moment when eleven days are destroyed.

HUDSON: You will never find rest – provided your beliefs, as expressed in your elegy, have any validity. It will be an eternal torment, loose, lost outside any hour, any memory.

GRAY: And never needed.

HUDSON:Never!

GRAY: Your revenge is badly designed, my lord. Sales of my poem have shot up during this turmoil over the lost days. People love me because I haven't meddled with Time but paid it a proper respect, as the government should. You will be ending my life at the zenith of my fame.That means I will stand more chance of being remembered. You would be granting me an everlasting glory.

* * *

A dishcloth hung between two six-inch nails is a work of art because Picasso said so. Experiment at the same challenging level has not been a feature of radio drama. In general experimental radio theatre is limited to rare breakthrough structures, such as *Under Milk Wood* and its impression of a piled-up, seething little town full of yearnings and dreams. *Under Milk Wood's* narrative is simply that of one day in the collective life of a community, with no climax or dénouement. Dylan Thomas wrote the play as a poet, and it works as poetry plus a documentary element – an unusual combination today but not so in the war years when artists served a function backed by government. I made an experiment in 1990 with a play called *Glossomaniacs*, directed by Martin Jenkins. It dealt with a mild psychosis I had noted on the increase over the previous ten years – people not being able to stop talking, a condition beyond mere garrulousness. There have always been a fair number of these psychotics in my circle of friends, acquaintances and relatives. I can sit at a bar or in a room, or be at the end of a telephone, and someone will talk for an hour without any need for a contribution from me. In some chronic cases I am able to leave the phone and go away for five minutes and on my return the caller will still be talking, having not needed any response. It is clear that being such a victim implies cowardice on my part – and cruelty for letting them indulge their psychosis. I pay the ear-tax too readily but there is a reason – I might be missing something.

For the purposes of revenge I based the characters on four glossomaniacs I know well. They are invited to dinner at the home of their psychiatrist in Hampstead. The doorbell rings, the psychiatrist can be heard walking down the hall to open it. Before she can say anything, the first glossomaniac starts talking. Then the second, third, and fourth arrive in order, until all four are around the dinner table going hammer and tongues.

Phrases underlined in the script rise above the sea of human sound, tempting the mind to grasp at narrative straws, to follow stories that then sink away. The effect is like one of those animated drinks parties in a small room where one stands in the door, amazed at the blasting strangeness of human speech.

Then one glossomaniac feels unwell and slides into incoherence, grinding eventually to a halt, followed by the others in sequence until there is a long blissful silence, broken by a brief laugh from the psychiatrist who, after too many years of having to be a good listener and being taken for granted, has poisoned them all.

Glossomaniacs is a revenge play. It only lasts for five minutes, but the auditory pain is intense. I rang my four friends and carefully slid the transmission date and time into the call. After the broadcast, two of them rang to say how they knew people just like that. The model for Max, a Cumbrian farmer who lived alone at eleven hundred feet with only sheep to talk to, told me the best way to deal with glossomaniacs was to tell them to shut up.

A German radio production of the play goes on for nine and a half minutes because the language takes much longer to say everything. This is too much agony for the average person. Five minutes is the maximum anyone can bear, even though people will endure several hours of such bombardment at a party without complaint, thinking they're having one hell of a time.

This leads me to think that the result of the experiment was to prove how art is definitely not life.

One enjoyable feature of this sado-masochistic outing was a generous act by the BBC, prompted, I suspect, by the good nature of the director, regardless of the enormous technical headache I'd given him. Because writers are paid an individual rate by the minute, it was decided I should receive four times my rate because the overlapping dialogue spoken by the characters was effectively four plays in one.

* * *

There are limits to the radio play. The cliché is that a writer can go anywhere, do anything with the form – but although that is theoretically the case, it is a freedom we sheer away from, compelled from within and without to observe the trammels of a certain as yet undefined social decency.

* * *

Visiting Thoor Ballyleee, the tower bought by W.B.Yeats in Galway as a symbol he could actually live in, which is now a museum, I was amazed to discover that the people running the place had no knowledge of his recorded reading of *The Lake Isle of Innisfree.* When I got home I made a copy of my cassette and sent it to them. A man as obsessed with the occult and the spirit world as Yeats deserves to have his voice back from the dead intoning magisterially inside his symbol. He never doubted the existence of the afterworld and incorporated technology into his system of mystic controls and agencies from the beyond. I'm surprised he never ventured into science fiction, which often marries the supernatural with machinery. He had H.G. Wells showing the way, after all. Perhaps pagan folklore, necromancy, magic, astrology, receiving gnomic dictation from the other side, and immense complexity in all things, was enough for him. Anyway, a great poet emerged from the confusion somehow. He received the Nobel Prize for Literature but should have been given another for obscurantism to go along with it.

At the time of writing, I'm researching the relationship between Yeats and Maud Gonne, the great Irish Republican beauty who starred in his short play *Cathleen ni Houlihan* in 1902 that inspired the heroes of the Easter Rising fourteeen years later. No other piece of theatre has such a direct line drawn from its performance to significant political action that shaped the future. The only play to come near it is Shakespeare's *Richard II*, written in 1594. Seven years later agents of the Earl of Essex commissioned a production of this piece about the deposition of a monarch to coincide with Essex's uprising against Queen Elizabeth. Essex and his supporters were executed. Shakespeare, like Yeats, was not included in the condemnation, though both could have suffered under less tolerant regimes. Productions of *Macbeth* were banned in the Russian empire in the nineteenth century because the murder of Duncan might encourage Anarchists to have a go at the Tsar. Come to think of it, half of Shakespeare's tragedies and histories are about the murder or deposition of kings…Hamlet, Lear, Richard III, Henry VI parts one, two and three…Julius Caesar can be thematically included…

Playwrights are intrigued by upset apple carts in no matter what manifestation. The same applies to people in power, provided it doesn't affect themselves.

Now the dust has settled on the political aspect of the debate, it seems to have been agreed that provided art predominates in the writing, the power of drama to provoke political action is solely in the individual mind of each member of the audience. The position previously occupied by hypersensitive imperial governments has been taken by violent religious opposition to theatre productions that are deemed to be insulting. Whereas the governments had the backing of secular laws on treason, the religious groups of today have only their subjective interpretation of what constitutes insult and heresy. These judgements are never reinforced by a central religious authority, although these same authorities often fail to condemn the action that closes the play.

No stage play under this kind of attack is ever adapted and broadcast as radio drama while it is hot news. If this ever happened, which is most unlikely given BBC policy, it would be interesting to find out whether the protests had the same strength. Once a radio play has been broadcast the experience is over, unlike a stage play running in a theatre which continues to pose a problem with each performance. The radio play exists as a recording but repeats are uncommon. At the moment the sectaries are in the ascendant, the government in a state of perpetual anxiety, and it is difficult at the moment to imagine how this can change.

There have been radio plays originating in the Manchester/ Leeds belt that deal directly with contemporary problems of Muslim extremism and non-integration. The ones I have heard have been impressively robust while ultimately fair-minded, written by playwrights of British Muslim background who seem, voluntarily or otherwise, bound by the BBC ethic of impartiality.

* * *

In spite of impressions that it was otherwise, radio was the voice of the terrible twentieth century. If its theatre had ever pentrated to the black depths of horror real events provided, no one would have listened because that's the way we are. Instead we go to the nihilism of Becket, which is superb on radio, perhaps the best way to experience it, or orchestrated banality of Pinter, heard on top of a bus. They help us avoid the great abyss by taking us near the edge, but the step back is easily taken. Absurdist humour enables us to appreciate what is meaningless but skilfully patterned so the mind can follow into the gentlest of despair, lulled by verbal wine. Perhaps all art recoils from the bottom of the pit where there is no light.

But is the human animal still listening with the same ears, or has our hearing been altered by overuse? Have there been too many voices put into our heads, too much music, too many sound effects of catastrophe and war?

Is there a reason why, by nature, we are not able to hear as much as our dogs? Was it always the case? Or has human hearing degenerated from that of the killer-ape roaming the African savannah in search of prey? In designing a radio play is there any other level to put the audience on than the floor of the common denominator?

* * *

Chapter VI

IT WAS ALWAYS intended that that the BBC should defend, help and promote the arts. I have been strongly supported by the BBC during my writing life. Without that support, maintaining a freelance existence as an author and not doing work of any other kind – journalism, teaching etc. – would at certain stages not been possible. In terms of the history of the arts in this country, the BBC has been a great patron, asking for nothing back but the work of the artist, which it pays for. No other country has a tax-fed patron of this kind, bureaucratic but creative and productive. Foreign writers envy our good fortune.

The bond created in my case has been through directors, seldom management because they work at a necessary distance, preferring to keep well in the background. Part of the job of directors is to protect authors from attempts at prescription and censorship, carrying on a tradition of keeping the BBC a congenial place for writers to work in. This bond involves fellowship, as well as corporate patronage, and has real meaning. It was damaged during the modernisation of the BBC's internal structure when reforms were imposed on the production of plays that proved insensitive and led to the alienation of writers. The result was to undermine the status of artistic endeavour, a heresy against BBC liberal doctrine, but that damage can easily be undone, if the will is there.

* * *

The BBC is at its weakest when it imitates commercial rivals. Within its known strengths and traditions it remains very powerful, capable of the highest sophistication and quality, with much superb achievement. There are times when one is in awe of the width and depth of what is offered to the listener and, if this is linked to its power as defender of an elemental political principle – the freedom *to think* within a balanced, impartially presented living environment – that means a great deal in the modern world. Lip-service to this ideal is paid throughout the media but everyone is aware that it is part of the BBC's *raison d'etre,* why and how it came into being.

Impartiality within the British Empire, or any empire come to that, was always a bit of a joke, and even inside BBC management impartiality often ceased to exist in pure form during the crises of war. However, the flame of impartiality, although it fluttered in the wind, never went out, and the shrine built around it became more solid. The BBC and impartiality are spoken of in the same breath today, as if one defines the other. The implication that a great intellectual ideal is embedded in a modern corporation is almost a contradiction in terms, but enough has happened to keep it credible. However, we don't need the BBC to be impartial *about itself.*

The BBC has never got off the tightrope of non-partisanship but should it come under direct threat in its present form, which seems ominously close in a time of brutal cuts to government-funded bodies, it will need partisans to fight for it. That fight will include the defence of radio theatre, which not only has a history of achievement in the mainstream of our culture, but also an immense future opening up just as the threat to its existence becomes acute.

* * *

Common or artistic sense does not prevail in oversized organisations. A lot of creative energy goes into making all the component parts mesh together in some semblance of productive unity. This requires conformity of practice and purpose. Often it appears that keeping the shape of the systems is of more importance than the function for which the company exists.

This classic, self-defeating dilemma became acute in the mid-nineties when the BBC was revamped from top to bottom to make it more efficient. Cutting-edge business methods were introduced departments right across the board – including those responsible for the production of original plays.

Conversely, the radio play entered a five-year period when it flourished and playwrights could do good work in a genuinely creative atmosphere. Whether this was due to BBC management policy, compensating for the killing off of one dramatic form – the single television play – by advancing another, I don't know.

If you have a company that makes a wide variety of goods it is bad practice to look upon them all as essentially the same thing. A manufacturer tooling up to make many different products doesn't put them all on the same line of machinery. That's a recipe for confusion, breakdowns and inferior work. Light entertainment and serious drama have some similar aspects but those aspects don't go very deep. Each needs special treatment within the traditions that have arisen during the active life of our culture. When playwrights of reputation with track records and achievements to their names discovered that a biography had to be submitted with each idea for a play as if every writer must be treated as an unknown, they naturally concluded that the people running the system were ignorant of the world they were being paid to have knowledge of – that of the writing of plays, and the means by which authors live – one of these being hard-won reputation. Henceforth, the credit of the Radio Drama Department – always very high amongst authors because of the deep experience, talent and knowledge therein, took a dive.

The systems imposed by higher management of the BBC on the Radio Drama Department were designed to exert control over creative forces that only flourish where such control is as light as possible. The conformity required to make the systems work was alien, taking the ease and naturalness out of relationships with playwrights.

To undo this frustrating management system and get everyone back into the flexible, human business of getting the best work out of our radio playwrights is not beyond the powers of the BBC. People of talent and insight are still within the department, if only they can be liberated from the heaviness of the corporate hand.

* * *

Talking down is common in radio drama. Perhaps this has been the bugbear from the start – underestimating the audience. The early BBC policy-makers were emphatic that plays putting the average mind under pressure were not wanted. What is odd about our own times is the way outspoken challenges to the most sensitive areas of thought have been taken away from playwrights and entrusted to comedians. If I put forward a play that would attack organised religion with the same scornful verve as Jeremy Hardy does on Radio 4, it would never be commissioned. This may be because the comedian always has the defence of saying he wasn't being serious. Playwrights can't use that excuse.

One can sit and watch film or television teeming with the worst kind of bad language and acts of bloodshed and sex. But if the same story was told on radio it would automatically be cleaned up. The radio audience is protected – even though it is the same audience as for film and television. The afternoon radio listener can be the late-night television watcher. The media-hungry spread themselves over the day. It is nothing to do with children. It is everything to do with the status of the mind. Insults to the eye do not register to the same degree. The ear is thought to be more delicate.

Giving special moral protection to the listenership has become rather a poignant question – poignant because though it lacks debate or awareness yet it seems rather sweet that the housewife with children listening to the afternoon play is still, in this raucous day and age, being sheltered. What is being said here? The underlying fact is that to keep the holy cow of the radio audience sacred while the Augean stables of the screen remain uncleansed is a response to a separation in the minds of our culture managers. Although decadence and corruption may run riot for the entertainment of the eye, the ear is a special case. Does the watcher need to avoid thought and the listener to avoid being taken too far by imagination? After forty years of writing radio plays I must admit to being confused – both on the issue of how and why this irrationality is maintained and what would happen if the censorship were removed.

In BBC radio any director of a play has to submit an application to a special watchdog if the use of a questionable word or phrase is required. This includes the tamest, most weak-hearted bad language in the canon. While some detective is fucking and blinding his way through a television series, his opposite number on radio is governed by the standards of fifty years ago, kept in place by responses to programmes by sections of the public. I'm not favouring a policy of opening the floodgates, but I suspect that the corporation's pressure on radio writing to conform and be prescribed is something to do with money and power rather than sense.

Overfame seldom touches the theatre of the ear. A star in a radio play shines in a very limited firmament. But there is no reason why radio drama should not reconquer the world. There is some watery evidence that it is on the upsurge, thanks to iPod technology. Once nausea reduces mass television audiences, radio can reclaim its massive pre-fifties following. Because it is proof against the worst excesses of fashion, a stern judge of bad writing and acting, people living under our global mediaocracy may increasingly turn to radio theatre as a dependable, sane partner in the life of the future.

Every art needs its uniqueness. Sound theatre has fused with something unusual – a corporation, and the uniqueness is shared because the BBC is as unique as radio theatre is. The theatre of the ear cannot survive without the care and support of one huge publicly funded body, which is also a national conscience. It's a very strange situation indeed – very British with Soviet overtones. The BBC effectively manages and sets the standards of the radio theatre of the English language and with it the world. There is no real competition.

* * *

Much of our new theatre from the subsidised sector became a form of political journalism in the Seventies, and remains so. This development was encouraged by university English and Theatre departments because here, at last, was structure to be studied. At the same time, Creative Writing became a university degree subject. Paines Plough, the national new play touring company we founded in 1975, is on tour this year with the work of *seventy-four* new playwrights, which is an astonishing number. That all are thoroughly workshopped and processed through active, open discussion is a fair assumption. Considering this background of education and training, is there any real unconditioned freedom left for a new writer out of nowhere who simply wants to make plays and get them produced? The best advice would be to form your own company and get on with it, but under current conditions that would be a long, long shot. With the interlocking circles within our culture management also exerting their weird powers, the amount of conformity required, often disguised as only reasonable, is too much for natural growth of a creative mind. Some anarchy needs to remain in the system.

BBC Radio could provide remedy from this exclusion by making a special slot available to the rank outsider, the voice from the wilderness. They must still be out there, somewhere, going mad in their isolation.

* * *

Anyone wanting to keep up with contemporary developments in the theatre during the eighties and nineties need only keep an ear cocked to Radio 3 and 4 to be in touch. The BBC's unwritten policy was to keep the different arts running alongside each other in broadcasting terms, showing the importance of interaction, providing a sense of movement and energy. No playwright active in the world was excluded, even those considered obscure and difficult.

This policy demonstrated a global interest rather than any UK parochialism. It harks back to the founding principles of the BBC and was part of the homogeneous core of strength that kept it upright in the mind of the public.

* * *

Chapter VII

IN THE BRITISH Library Sound Archive is a wealth of radio plays by our best writers – poets, playwrights, and novelists. The moment is approaching when this has to be less of a secret store open only to the researcher who will take the trouble to go to the building, borrow the tape and play it on the premises. Why should these plays be left unheard by the general public at a time when the listenership is expanding? We are able to watch old classic films, why should the best radio plays of the past not be available to us? As the pattern of listening changes, opening up and increasing the audience by means of podcasting and the internet, we should be able to enjoy that great archive, including the experimental and the difficult, even the impossible. It is known that the BBC periodically culled its tape archive since World War II, taking informed decisions on whether to preserve recordings according to the quality of work and the reputation of authors and actors. Those selections need to be kept up to date and include the work of all the independent companies that produce radio plays for the BBC. At the moment they appear to be excluded from the process.

* * *

Not someone to turn away from good fortune, or keep its magic to myself, I pass on a marvellous synchronicity that occurred literally as I was getting ready to write the end of this book. After some thought I decided the synchronicity had a revelation hidden inside it and should take its place as the true end of what I have to say.

The first radio play to be commissioned and broadcast in Britain was *Danger* by poet, playwright and novelist Richard Hughes, a Surrey-born writer, Charterhouse and Oxford, known to be highly original and idiosyncratic. (This conflicts with subsequent BBC policy that radio drama should not be difficult for the average mind). The half-hour play concerned a group of Welsh coal miners trapped underground. It was transmitted by the BBC on January 15th 1924. Later it was revived and put on disc under the title *The Birth of Radio Drama,* which is innacurate because plays transmitted in the USA on commercial radio stations preceeded it by a couple of years.

On today's BBC news first thing there was a report from a gold and copper mine in the Atacama Desert of northern Chile, of thirty-three men trapped by a rockfall in a space the size of an average one bedroom flat at a depth of two thousand feet. Telephone contact has been made via three narrow ventilation shafts which are big enough, however, to send down food and water supplies. When the telephone link was first made the miners sang the Chilean national anthem.

It is estimated that it will take four months to drill a shaft the circumference of a bicycle wheel to rescue them. Miners who are overweight will have to diet in order to get up the shaft. The problem of extracting those who are simply too broad in the shoulder or waistline to fit through is being thought about.

Anti-depressant tablets have been sent down. There will be much counselling. The families of the men are camped out at the shaft-head and intend to wait out the four months. One family has already started legal proceedings because the pit was declared unsafe in the past, closed down, then re-opened with the approval of the ministry of mines.

The San José mining company has apologised for the accident.

NASA has given advice on how the miners should stay sane, based on the routines of astronauts living in space stations.

The world media with their cameras and microphones will be camped alongside the families for as long as the news has any heat in it, which may be a surprisingly short period. Global news reporting is notoriously fickle because other catastrophes queue up to happen.

If he were alive, and commissioned again by the BBC, what would Richard Hughes, that original and idiosyncratic playwright of 1924, make of San José in 2010? His mine in *Danger,* was a simple, elemental place, close to Hell, where death breathed in the darkness. The San José mine is a paradigm of twenty-first century interconnectedness, a parable of how we are buried in cyberspace where anything can happen. Those men in their one-bedroom flat far under the earth represent our computer-dominated world, hanging on to its humanity by its fingertips, seemingly infinite in concept but claustrophobically small in truth. To write a play for modern listeners Hughes would have to work his way through wider, deeper, stranger, and more frightening issues than death.

* * *

The primary school is a hundred yards up the road. At three-fifteen each afternoon during term-time the silence of this hill village is swept away by the voices of children chattering as they meet their mothers or wander off to homes nearby. Next door to where I'm writing is a Congregational chapel. At ten o'clock every Sunday the silence is raggedly removed by the first hymn. As an ex-choirboy I once knew them all by heart and test my memory by singing along under my breath. On Saturdays at six in the evening, which is quiet, quiet, quiet here on the edge of the valley, the bell-ringers practice their permutations in the tower of Saint Mary the Virgin down the road, calling changes. Every Wednesday fortnight at eight in the morning the bin-men come for the bottles and each crash outside each house tells its story. At set times in the routine of a civilised life there are also radio plays for the asking, plays that can move any silence aside with art, force and meaning, plays that demand one of the higher unselfish talents we look for in each other – that of being a good listener.

Saint Briavels, September 2010

David Pownall

Also Available from Oberon

The Dream of Chief Crazy Horse

£7.99 / 978-1-84002-075-5

Getting the Picture

£7.99 / 978-1-84002-007-6

Innocent Screams

£8.99 / 978-1-84002-611-5

Nijinsky: Death of a Faun

£7.99 / 978-1-84002-000-7

Collections:

Plays One

An Audience Called Edouard, Livingstone and Sechele, Motocar, Richard III Part Two

£9.99 / 978-1-84002-076-2

Plays Two

Beef, The Viewing, My Father's House, Black Star

£12.99 / 978-1-84002-077-9

The Composer Plays

Master Class, Elgar's Rondo, Music to Murder By, Elgar's Third

£9.99 / 978-1-870259-41-5

Lancaster Plays

Gaunt, Lile Jimmy Williamson, Buck Ruxton, A Tale of Two Town Halls

£14.99 / 978-1-84002-644-3

Plays for One Person

Crates on Barrels, Later, Rousseau's Tale

£9.99 / 978-1-84002-010-6

Radio Plays

An Epiphanous Use of the Microphone, Beef, Flas, Ploughboy Monday, Under the Table, Kitty Wilkinson

£9.99 / 978-1-84002-034-2

Other titles in the Oberon Masters Series include:

The Art of Translation - Ranjit Bolt

£9.99 / 978-1-84002-865-2

Exposed by the Mask - Peter Hall

£9.99 / 978-1-84002-993-2

The Role of the Critic - Nicholas Dromgoole

£9.99 / 978-1-84002-973-4

Sound of Musicals - Ruth Leon

£9.99 / 978-1-84943-018-0

To Set Prometheus Free - A.C. Grayling

£9.99 / 978-1-84002-962-8

Against All Gods - A.C. Grayling

£9.99 / 978-1-84002-728-0

Theatre and the Mind - Mick Gordon

£9.99 / 978-1-84002-876-8

Wesker on Theatre - Arnold Wesker

£9.99 / 978-1-84002-986-4